John F Kennedy

History Makers

D0709901

Jane Sutcliffe

Lerner

LERNER BOOKS • LONDON • NEW YORK • MINNEAPOLIS

For Rose G. McCormick, who first taught me about John F Kennedy.

Illustrations by Tim Parlin

First published in the United Kingdom in 2008 by
Lerner Books,
Dalton House,
60 Windsor Avenue,
London SW19 2RR

Website address: www.lernerbooks.co.uk

This edition was updated and edited for UK publication by Discovery Books Ltd., Unit 3, 37 Watling Street, Leintwardine, Shropshire SY7 0LW

British Library Cataloguing in Publication Data

Sutcliffe, Jane
  John F. Kennedy. - (History makers)
  1. Kennedy, John F. (John Fitzgerald), 1917-1963 - Juvenile
  literature 2. Presidents - United States - Biography -
  Juvenile literature 3. United States - Politics and
  government - 1961-1963 - Juvenile literature
  I. Title
  973.9'22'092

  ISBN-13: 978 1 58013 449 1

Printed in China

TABLE OF CONTENTS

INTRODUCTION

John F Kennedy was the thirty-fifth president of the United States of America. Not everyone thought he would make a good president. Some people thought he was too young. Others said his religion was a problem.

President Kennedy worked hard to prove those people wrong. He led the United States during a dangerous time. He won the respect of the world. Then suddenly he was gone. His death shocked and saddened people everywhere.

This is his story.

1 A 'MUCKER' GROWS UP

John F Kennedy was not supposed to grow up to become president. His brother Joe was. At least that's what their father had decided. When Joseph Kennedy Senior decided something, that was that.

John was born on 29 May 1917, in Brookline, Massachusetts. His father was a wealthy businessman. His mother was the daughter of the mayor of Boston.

John was named after his grandfather, John Fitzgerald, but everyone called him Jack. Jack was the second of nine Kennedy children. Joe was the first. All the Kennedy children liked sports and games. They raced sailing boats and played rough games of American football. They always played to win. 'We don't want any losers around here,' their father said. 'In this family, we want winners.'

The Kennedy family in 1932 (LEFT TO RIGHT): Bobby, Jack, Eunice, Jean, Mr and Mrs Kennedy, Patricia, Kathleen, Joe Jnr and Rosemary. Brother Teddy came along later.

Sometimes Jack couldn't play. He was ill much of the time. He had high fevers, his back hurt and his stomach bothered him.

Being ill so often made Jack skinny. Despite this he was a handsome boy. He had blue eyes and thick sandy hair. When he laughed, his wide smile seemed to spread over his whole face.

A TIE RACE

Jack and his brother Joe were always daring each other. Once they had a race around the neighbourhood on their bikes. They set off in opposite directions. At the finish, they sped towards each other head-on. Neither would slow down or turn! The race ended in a nasty crash. Jack needed twenty-eight stitches.

Jack (RIGHT) poses
with a few of his
fellow muckers.

When he was fourteen, Jack went away to secondary school. Joe was already there. The school had a lot of rules. Rules didn't bother Joe at all and he did well at school. Jack was different. He hated rules and was always late for lessons. His room was a mess and his marks were terrible.

The headmaster had a name for students like Jack. He called them 'muckers'. Jack didn't mind being called a mucker. In fact, he and his friends formed the Muckers Club. Soon there were over a dozen members.

Mostly, the boys just met in Jack's room and listened to music. Then a rumour went around the school. The Muckers were going to smuggle a pile of horse manure into a school dance. They were going to dump it right onto the dance floor!

The headmaster heard the rumour. That was the end of the Muckers Club. The headmaster called Jack's father to the school. Mr Kennedy wasn't happy that his son was in trouble, but he was proud of Jack too. He saw that Jack had been a leader to the other boys.

Jack studied political science at Harvard University. He played American football and joined the swimming team.

Jack (RIGHT) and Joe Jnr (LEFT) arrived in England with their father (CENTRE) in the summer of 1938.

After he left secondary school, Jack became a student at Harvard University. Then Jack's father got an important job in England. Jack took time off from Harvard to join his family there.

In 1939 Europe was heading for war. Jack travelled all over Europe. He wanted to see for himself what was going on. When he returned to Harvard, he wrote a long essay about what he had seen. Jack's professors liked his ideas. The paper helped Jack to graduate from Harvard with honours.

Jack's father thought the essay would make a good book. With the help of friends, Jack's book was published in 1940. It was called *Why England Slept* and was a big success.

By 1941, Jack was twenty-four. He was a Harvard graduate. He was a best-selling author and he was the son of a very wealthy man. Jack could have done just about anything. He decided to join the US Navy. The Second World War was already being fought in Europe. Jack knew that soon the United States would have to join the war too. He wanted to help his country when that happened.

2 PT-109

Bombs! Jack heard the word on the radio. Japanese planes had bombed the US naval base at Pearl Harbor, Hawaii. The United States of America was at war.

Jack was sent to the Solomon Islands, in the Pacific Ocean. He took command of a small, flimsy wooden boat called a PT boat. The PT stood for 'patrol torpedo'. Jack's boat was *PT-109*.

The little boats patrolled the waters at night. The crew looked for enemy ships. Then they torpedoed and sank them. That was the way it was supposed to work, but on many nights Jack and his crew saw no enemy ships at all.

In the early morning of 2 August 1943, *PT-109* was on patrol as usual. There was no moon. It was so dark that the crew could barely see each other, let alone a passing ship.

Jack (FAR RIGHT) poses with his crew aboard PT-109.

Jack's crew was constantly on the lookout for Japanese destroyers such as this one. The crew's job was to fire on the enemy ships and sink them.

Out of the darkness, an enemy destroyer appeared! The ship ran straight into the side of *PT-109*. With a roar, the boat's fuel tanks exploded. The ship continued through the fireball, nearly cutting the PT boat in half.

Two of Jack's men were killed in the crash. The rest had to swim for an island six kilometres away. One of the men was badly burned. He couldn't swim, so Jack took the strap from the man's life jacket and put it between his teeth. Then he began swimming, towing the man along with him.

When they got to the island, the men were exhausted. Jack was exhausted too. Even so, that night he swam back out to look for a rescue ship, but he saw nothing.

For the next three days, Jack swam from island to island looking for help. At last, he met two local people. They agreed to carry a message for Jack. Of course, Jack didn't have any paper, so he used a knife to carve his message on a coconut.

Jack's unusual message worked. Six days after the crash, the crew was rescued. Jack was awarded the Navy and Marine Corps Medal for his bravery, but he hated being called a hero. He said, 'The real heroes are not the men who return, but those who stay out there . . . two of my men included.'

THE COCONUT IN THE WHITE HOUSE

Jack held on to his lucky coconut shell. When he became president, it sat on his desk in the White House (the official home of the president of the United States).

Captain F L Conklin presents the Navy and Marine Corps Medal to Jack in 1944.

Jack's health had always been bad. After the shipwreck, it got worse. He was skinnier than ever. His back hurt so badly that he needed a cane to walk. The navy sent him home. In June 1944, Jack had surgery on his back. Then he went to his family's home to rest.

He was there when the Kennedys received some terrible news. Jack's brother Joe had been killed in the war.

Everyone, especially Jack's father, had expected Joe to become a famous politician. Now Joe was gone, Mr Kennedy began to focus on Jack instead. Jack too, began to think about a life in politics.

THE CAMPAIGN TRAIL

In 1946 the state of Massachusetts needed a new representative in the US Congress. Jack's father wanted him to run for the office. Jack liked the idea too, but there was just one problem. None of the voters knew who Jack was, so his family went to work.

Jack's father used his money to buy advertising. Jack's mother and sisters held tea parties to introduce Jack to the voters.

Jack worked hardest of all. He went to factories, fire stations and pool halls to meet voters. He gave hundreds of speeches. Many people liked his relaxed, easy way of speaking.

His father was surprised. He saw that Jack had a natural gift for politics.

When Jack first started running for office in 1946, he was a little shy. Still, he kept giving speeches and soon it was clear that he had a passion for politics.

Jack won the election easily. The voters must have liked Representative Kennedy because they re-elected him twice. In 1952, he ran for the US Senate. When he won that election he became Senator Kennedy.

One night at a dinner party, Jack met Jacqueline Bouvier. 'Jackie' was young, smart and elegant. Jack had dated many pretty women, but he had never met

anyone like Jackie. Jack and Jackie dated for almost a year. On 12 September 1953, they were married.

Jackie was beautiful and smart. She had gone to school in Paris and spoke four languages.

PROFILES IN COURAGE quickly became a best-seller. Jack often signed copies of the book for his fans.

The Kennedys had not been married long when Jack needed another operation on his back. This one went badly, Jack took months to recover. He used his time to write another book. The book told the stories of eight brave Americans, including the 6th president, John Quincy Adams. Jack called it *Profiles in Courage.*

Jack and Jackie's first child, Caroline, was born in 1957. Caroline was a delight to her proud parents. They spent as much time with her as they could.

The book won an important award, the Pulitzer Prize, and earned Jack a lot of attention. In 1956, Jack was nearly picked as a candidate for vice president, but he lost the vote. He knew that with hard work, he could go even further. In January 1960, Jack announced that he would run for president of the United States.

Jack knew that he was not the ideal candidate for president. One problem was his age. Jack was only forty-three. Some people thought that he was too young, but other voters liked the idea of a young president. They saw that Jack was bursting with energy, and he promised to 'get the country moving'.

Jack ran for president in 1960. Whenever he gave a speech, large crowds came to hear him.

A Secret

When Jack was thirty, doctors were finally able to tell him why he was ill so often. He had an illness called Addison's disease. Jack had to take medicine for the rest of his life. No one outside his family knew this, though. Jack and his family kept his illness a secret.

Jack's religion was another problem. He was Catholic. The leader of the Roman Catholic Church is the pope, who lives in Rome. The pope is in charge of Catholics all over the world. Some people thought that the pope shouldn't tell a president of the United States what to do. There had never been a Catholic president before. These people wanted to keep it that way.

Jack went on television. He spoke about his religion. He stood up for his right to be president. After all, 'nobody asked me if I was Catholic when I joined the United States Navy,' he said.

At last, Jack was named the Democratic Party's choice for president. The Republican Party chose Richard Nixon. Jack would have to beat Nixon to become president.

Jack asked Nixon to take part in a debate. The two would discuss important issues face-to-face. The debate was the first ever seen on television. Millions of people watched. Most of them thought that Nixon looked nervous. There were little beads of sweat on his upper lip. Jack, on the other hand, looked calm. He seemed sure of his answers. That's how a president should look, viewers said.

This family watches the debate between Jack Kennedy and Richard Nixon. Most people thought Jack looked good on television.

On 8 November 1960, Americans voted. It was very close, but when all the votes were counted, Jack had made history. He was the youngest person – and the first Roman Catholic – ever to be elected as president of the United States of America.

A PRESIDENT'S JOB

Jack and Jackie moved into the White House, in Washington DC, with their two children. Caroline was three years old. Her little brother, John Jnr, was just a baby.

Straight away, Jack started a programme called the Peace Corps. Peace Corps volunteers went to poor countries. They helped to train teachers, and they taught people how to build roads and plant crops.

Peace Corps volunteers live in villages with the people they are trying to help. They learn the people's language and customs.

Soon thousands of Peace Corps volunteers were making friends for the United States all around the world.

Sometimes Jack had to deal with countries that did not like the United States of America. The most powerful of these countries was the Soviet Union. The two countries were not at war, but they were not at peace either. People called it the 'Cold War'. Jack had to make sure that the Cold War did not turn into a real war.

One morning, an assistant showed Jack some photographs. The pictures showed that the Soviet Union was putting missiles on the island of Cuba. Cuba was only 145 kilometres away from the United States. Jack knew that this was a big problem. A nuclear missile fired from Cuba could reach an American city in minutes.

NUCLEAR WARHEAD BUNKER
UNDER CONSTRUCTION
SAN CRISTOBAL SITE 1

PREFABRICATION MATERIALS

A spy plane took this photo of a missile site that the Soviet Union was building in Cuba.

Jack's advisers helped him decide what to do about the missiles in Cuba.

The missiles had to be taken away, but how could he make that happen? His advisers wanted him to send planes to attack Cuba, and to destroy the missiles. Of course, any Soviets working on the missiles would be killed and that would start a nuclear war with the Soviet Union. A war like that had never been fought before. Half the people in the United States could die!

Instead, Jack decided to 'quarantine' Cuba. US Navy ships would surround the island and make a blockade. They would stop Soviet ships from reaching Cuba and delivering more missiles.

Jack hoped that the blockade would prevent a deadly war. No one was quite sure what the Soviets would do. They might become so angry that they would fire their missiles anyway. The blockade might start a war after all!

On 24 October 1962 the blockade began. Over 170 US ships were already in place around Cuba. Soviet ships steamed towards them. What would happen when the two sides met? All Jack could do was wait.

'WE CHOOSE TO GO TO THE MOON'

Soon after Jack became president, the Soviets launched the first person into space. Jack didn't like coming in second to the Soviets. He promised that the United States of America would be first to land an astronaut on the Moon. The United States kept Jack's promise. On 20 July 1969, Neil Armstrong became the first person to walk on the Moon.

Before the missile crisis, Jack met with the leader of the Soviet Union. The two agreed on very little.

Suddenly, word came. The Soviet ships had stopped! They were not trying to cross the quarantine line. They were turning around. The blockade had worked!

Four days later, the Soviets agreed to remove the missiles from Cuba. Jack's gamble had paid off. The crisis was over.

Sometimes danger didn't come from other countries. Sometimes it came from the American people themselves.

In the South, black Americans were asking for more rights. They held marches in the streets. Some people didn't want black Americans to have the same rights as white Americans. There were riots. Police dogs attacked the black marchers. High-pressure hoses knocked them off their feet and angry crowds insulted them.

Three civil rights protesters are sprayed with a high-pressure fire hose. Its spray is strong enough to tear the bark from trees.

In June 1963 two black students tried to enroll at the University of Alabama. The school had never had a black student before. The governor of Alabama himself tried to stop the students. He stood in the doorway of the school and would not let them pass. It was an ugly moment. Jack had to send soldiers to end the stand-off. At last, the students were admitted.

Governor George Wallace blocks a doorway at the University of Alabama.

Jack told the American people that discrimination was wrong. Unfortunately not everyone agreed with him.

That night, Jack spoke to the country on television. He spoke plainly. He said that treating people differently because of the colour of their skin was wrong. He said it had no place in American law and should have no place in American life.

He told people that he was asking for new laws to be passed. The laws would make sure that all Americans – white or black – would be treated the same. It was not enough to change the law, he said. He challenged the American people to change their minds. He challenged them to change their lives.

Martin Luther King Jnr spoke to more than 250,000 people during the march on Washington.

Two months after Jack's speech, there was another march for equality. This one was in Washington, DC. Thousands of people gathered around the Lincoln Memorial. They cheered as they listened to speeches by black leaders. One of the speakers at the march was Martin Luther King Jnr. He stirred everyone who heard him with his 'I Have a Dream' speech. There were no riots and no fighting. Everything was peaceful.

After the march, Jack invited the leaders to the White House. He shook their hands. When he shook King's hand, Jack said, 'I have a dream.' It was Jack's way of saying that he had been moved by King's speech too. He told the leaders how happy he was with the march. 'You made the difference,' one told him. 'You gave us your blessings.'

Civil rights leaders meet with Jack in the White House. King is third from the left.

5 DALLAS

Not everyone was happy with the job that Jack was doing. Some were angry at what he had done for black Americans. Others wanted him to be tougher on the Soviet Union.

A new election was coming up. Jack was determined to win. That meant he would have to convince the voters that he was doing a good job.

Jack decided to start his election campaign in the southern states of the USA. On 22 November 1963, he and Jackie went to Dallas, Texas.

The crowd that greeted Jack's plane was happy to see him. People were jumping up and down in excitement. They screamed and cheered as if he were a rock star. Jack called it a 'real Texas welcome'.

Jack and Jackie receive a warm welcome in Dallas. Jackie carries a bouquet of red roses given to her upon her arrival.

Jackie greets an enthusiastic crowd in Dallas.

Jack and Jackie shook hands with some of the crowd. Then they stepped into an open car for the ride through Dallas. The governor of Texas and his wife joined them.

The streets of Dallas were lined with people – 250,000 of them. They jostled each other to get glimpses of Jack and Jackie. They leaned out of windows for a better view. The roar of their cheers drowned out the sound of the motorcycles riding alongside Jack's car.

Jack and Jackie ride through the streets of Dallas.

Crack!

Suddenly, a sharp noise echoed through the streets. A car backfiring, thought some people. Firecrackers, thought others.

But they were wrong. The sound was a gunshot. A bullet streaked over the heads of the crowd. It hit Jack. A moment later, another bullet followed. This one also struck him. Jack slumped to the side of his seat in the car. The governor of Texas was hit too.

The president had been shot! The car roared forwards. It raced to the hospital, but it was too late. A short time later, the official word came. At the age of forty-six, John F Kennedy was dead.

Radio and TV announcers told people what had happened. The nation was stunned by the horrible news. All over the country, people stopped what they were doing. For the rest of their lives, they would remember where they had been at that moment.

People all over the world mourned the death of Jack Kennedy.

The car that Jack rode in was specially made for the president of the United States of America. Officially, it was called X-100. After Jack died, four more presidents used the car — Lyndon B Johnson, Richard Nixon, Gerald Ford and Jimmy Carter. In 1977, the car went to the Henry Ford Museum. It was put on display as a piece of America's history.

John F Kennedy had been president for only 1,036 days. In that short time, he had made the country safer. He had set the nation on a new road towards equal rights for black Americans. He had encouraged Americans to aim for the Moon and the stars. He had opened a door to a new future for the American people, but they would have to meet that future without him. John F Kennedy was gone.

TIMELINE

In the year . . .

1935   John F Kennedy left secondary school.

1940   he graduated from Harvard University in June.
His book *Why England Slept* was published in August.

      Age 23

1941   he joined the US Navy in October.
The United States entered the Second World War on 8 December.

1943   *PT-109* was sunk on 2 August.

1946   Jack was first elected to the US House of Representatives.

      Age 29

1952   he was first elected to the US Senate.

1953   he married Jacqueline Bouvier on 12 September.

1956   his book *Profiles in Courage* was published.

1960   he was elected president of the United States of America.

      Age 43

1961   he created the Peace Corps.

1962   he announced a quarantine to end the Soviet shipment of missiles to Cuba.

1963   in June he announced new laws to give equal rights to black Americans.
He was killed in Dallas, Texas, on 22 November.
He was awarded the Presidential Medal of Freedom by President Johnson in December.

      Age 46

WHO KILLED THE PRESIDENT?

L ee Harvey Oswald was arrested for killing President
Kennedy. Two days later, he too was shot and killed.
There was no trial. So there was no way to judge what had
happened on 22 November 1963. Some people wondered
whether or not Oswald really was the killer.

Over the years, people have pointed fingers at all sorts of
suspects. Some said a group of criminals killed Kennedy.
Others said it was spies from a foreign country. Some even
said it was agents from the United States government itself.

No one has ever found anything to prove these stories.
All the evidence points to Oswald. Still, some people continue
to ask: Who really
killed John F
Kennedy?

*Lee Harvey Oswald
(RIGHT) was shot as
he was being moved to
a different prison on
24 November 1963.*

FURTHER READING

Anderson, Michael. *The Civil Rights Movement* (20th Century Perspectives) Heinemann Library, 2004.

Carter, E J. *The Cuban Missile Crisis* (20th Century Perspectives) Heinemann Library, 2004.

Chrisp, Peter. *Kennedy* (20th Century Leaders) Hodder Children's Books, 2002.

Dherbier, Yann-Brice and Pierre-Henri Verlhac. *John F. Kennedy: A Life in Pictures* Phaidon Press Ltd, 2003.

Malam, John. *First Man on the Moon: 21 July 1969* (Dates with History) Cherrytree Books, 2003.

Price Hossell, Karen. *I Have a Dream* (Voices of Freedom) Heinemann Library, 2006.

Price Hossell, Karen. *John F. Kennedy's Inaugural Speech* (Voices of Freedom) Heinemann Library, 2006.

Taylor, Davis. *The Cold War* (20th Century Perspectives) Heinemann Library, 2001.

Williams, Brian. *Assassination of President Kennedy: 22 November 1963* (Dates with History) Cherrytree Books, 2002.

WEBSITES

The White House: John Kennedy
<http://www.whitehouse.gov/history/presdents/jk35html>
Visitors to this website can learn about Jack's life.

The Peace Corps
<www.peacecorps.gov> Learn all about the Peace Corps at
this informative website, including where corps volunteers
work and what they do.

SELECT BIBLIOGRAPHY

Ballard, Robert D. 'The Search for PT-109.' *National
Geographic*, December 2002, 78–87.

Bishop, Jim. *The Day Kennedy Was Shot*. New York: Funk
& Wagnalls, 1968.

Dallek, Robert. 'The Medical Ordeals of JFK.' *Atlantic
Monthly*, December 2002, 49–61.

Hamilton, Nigel. *JFK: Reckless Youth*. New York: Random
House, 1992.

Kennedy, John F. *The Greatest Speeches of President John F.
Kennedy*. Bellingham, WA: Titan Publishing, 2001.

Kenney, Charles. *John F. Kennedy: The Presidential
Portfolio: History as Told through the Collection of the
John F. Kennedy Library and Museum*. New York:
PublicAffairs, 2000.

*Report of the President's Commission on the Assassination
of President Kennedy*. Washington, DC: US Government
Printing Office, 1964.

INDEX

Acknowledgements

For photographs and artwork: The John F Kennedy Library, pp 4, 7, 9, 10, 11, 14, 17, 19, 21, 23, 29, 30, 32, 35, 37, 39, 40; © CORBIS, p 15; *The New Bedford Standard-Times,* p 20; © Bettmann/CORBIS, pp 22, 33, 42; National Archives, p 25; The Peace Corps, p 28; © Hulton|Archive by Getty Images, p 34; © Hulton-Deutsch Collection/CORBIS, p 36; The Everett Collection, pp 41, 45; Front Cover: John F Kennedy Library; Back Cover: © David J and Janice L Frent Collection/CORBIS.

For quoted material: pp 7, 16, Nigel Hamilton, *JFK: Reckless Youth* (New York: Random House, 1992); pp 23, 24, 37, Charles Kenney, *John F. Kennedy: The Presidential Portfolio: History as Told through the Collection of the John F. Kennedy Library and Museum* (New York: PublicAffairs, 2000); p 30, *John F. Kennedy, The Greatest Speeches of President John F. Kennedy* (Bellingham, WA: Titan Publishing, 2001); p 37, Richard Reeves, *President Kennedy: Profile of Power* (New York: Simon & Schuster, 1993); p 39, Jim Bishop, *The Day Kennedy Was Shot* (New York: Funk & Wagnalls, 1968).